JOHN CONSTANTINE
HELLBLAZER

THE ROOTS OF COINCIDENCE

JOHN CONSTANTINE
HELLBLAZER

THE ROOTS OF COINCIDENCE

ANDY DIGGLE writer

The Mortification of the Flesh
Parts 1 and 2
Giuseppe Camuncoli penciller
Stefano Landini inker

The Roots of Coincidence
Parts 1, 2 and 3
Leonardo Manco artist

Lee Loughridge colorist

Jared K. Fletcher letterer

Lee Bermejo original series covers
with special thanks to Mauro Corrandini

KAREN BERGER Senior VP-Executive Editor   BOB SCHRECK CASEY SEIJAS Editors-original series
BRANDON MONTCLARE Assistant Editor-original series   BOB HARRAS Editor-collected edition
ROBBIN BROSTERMAN Senior Art Director   PAUL LEVITZ President & Publisher
GEORG BREWER VP-Design & DC Direct Creative   RICHARD BRUNING Senior VP-Creative Director
PATRICK CALDON Executive VP-Finance & Operations   CHRIS CARAMALIS VP-Finance   JOHN CUNNINGHAM VP-Marketing
TERRI CUNNINGHAM VP-Managing Editor   AMY GENKINS Senior VP-Business & Legal Affairs   ALISON GILL VP-Manufacturing
DAVID HYDE VP-Publicity   HANK KANALZ VP-General Manager, WildStorm   JIM LEE Editorial Director-WildStorm
GREGORY NOVECK Senior VP-Creative Affairs   SUE POHJA VP-Book Trade Sales   STEVE ROTTERDAM Senior VP-Sales & Marketing
CHERYL RUBIN Senior VP-Brand Management   ALYSSE SOLL VP-Advertising & Custom Publishing
JEFF TROJAN VP-Business Development, DC Direct   BOB WAYNE VP-Sales

Cover illustration by Lee Bermejo.

JOHN CONSTANTINE, THE ROOTS OF COINCIDENCE

FATHER GRIMALDI
CAN'T SLEEP.

THE MANY GATES OF THE
VATICAN CITY HAVE LONG SINCE
CLOSED, THE TEEMING HORDES
OF SIGHTSEERS AND PILGRIMS
USHERED OUT FOR THE NIGHT.

THESE HOURS ARE THE WORST
FOR HIM. THE DEEP WATCHES OF
THE NIGHT, WHEN THE HALLS AND
CORRIDORS OF THE APOSTOLIC PALACE
HAVE LONG SINCE FALLEN SILENT.

SILENT, BUT FOR
THE THING BEHIND
THE *DOOR.*

THREE DAYS IT HAS BEEN NOW.

THREE DAYS AND THREE NIGHTS SINCE HE LAST SLEPT, DOWN HERE IN THE GROTTOES BENEATH THE PALACE, IN THE SECLUDED CORRIDOR THAT HAS BECOME HIS HOME.

HE HAS CORDONED OFF THE APPROACHES, CLAIMING THE CELLARS ARE CLOSED FOR REFURBISHMENT. A FEEBLE DECEPTION THAT HE KNOWS CANNOT SUFFICE MUCH LONGER.

CHIUSO PER LAVORI

A COMFORTABLE BED AWAITS HIM IN THE APARTMENTS ABOVE. BUT HE DARE NOT LEAVE THE *DOOR* UNGUARDED.

SOMETHING *HEAVY* BUMPS AND SLITHERS AGAINST THE ANCIENT OAK. IT CANNOT HOLD FOREVER.

AND FATHER GRIMALDI KNOWS HIS TIME IS RUNNING OUT.

FOR THE THOUSANDTH TIME, HE CONSIDERS TAKING HIS OWN LIFE. BUT TO DO SO WOULD BE A *SIN* IN THE EYES OF GOD.

FOR THE THOUSANDTH TIME, HE REFLECTS UPON THE FACT THAT IT WOULD NOT BE A SIN IN THE *ROOM*...

...*BUT* HE CANNOT OPEN THE DOOR.

HE WOULD SMILE AT THE IRONY, IF HE WERE STILL CAPABLE.

THE THING IN THE ROOM BEGINS TO WHEEDLE AND CAJOLE, THEN ROARS LIKE A JUNGLE BEAST.

FATHER GRIMALDI PLUGS HIS EARS WITH CANDLE WAX AND DRAWS THE BLANKET ABOUT HIMSELF, THE MARBLE FLOOR COLD AND HARD BENEATH HIS SHOULDER.

HE STARES AT THE DOOR FOR SEVERAL HOURS BEFORE, FINALLY, HE SLIPS INTO A FITFUL SLEEP...

...AND HE DREAMS.

LOOK AT ME, LUIGI.

I--I DARE NOT... I AM *UNWORTHY!*

YOU ARE AS GOD *MADE* YOU, LUIGI. HOW COULD YOU BE UNWORTHY OF HIS LOVE?

I--I'M SO AFRAID! AFRAID FOR MY IMMORTAL *SOUL*...

HOW CAN GOD FORGIVE ME FOR WHAT I HAVE DONE...?

HE *IS* FORGIVENESS. YOU HAVE BUT TO OPEN YOUR HEART TO HIM.

YOU KNOW THE TRUTH OF THIS. HOW CAN YOU DOUBT IT?

FOR THERE IS NO ROOM FOR DOUBT, LUIGI, IN *THIS* HOUR ABOVE ALL OTHERS.

THE ENEMY IS AT THE GATE-- AND *YOU* HAVE BEEN APPOINTED TO STAND WATCH.

AND HE AWAKENS.

THE THING IN THE ROOM BEGINS TO SCREAM LIKE A CHILD, MINDLESS WITH TERROR. HE IMAGINES IT CLAWING AT THE DOOR WITH BLOODY FINGERNAILS.

AND HE REALIZES THAT, FOR THE FIRST TIME, IT IS *AFRAID.*

HE *RUNS* TO THE CONFESSIONAL WITH SOMETHING IN HIS HEART HE HAD THOUGHT *DEAD* NOW FOR THREE DAYS AND THREE NIGHTS.

HOPE.

THE SISTINE CHAPEL STANDS EMPTY AT THIS HOUR, SILENT IN ITS SPLENDOR.

SO MUCH THE BETTER.

HIS CONFESSION IS FOR GOD, AND GOD ALONE.

BUT-- BUT--

NICE CEILING. UNDERSTATED.

WHO'S YOUR DECORATOR?

THIS IS A HOUSE OF GOD, NOT A-- A *TOURIST TRAP!*

I'M CALLING FOR THE *SWISS GUARD,* THEY WILL ESCORT YOU FROM THE CHAPEL--

ALL RIGHT, *PADRE,* DON'T GET YOUR CASSOCK IN A TWIST. AFTER ALL...

...THERE'S NO NEED TO SHOOT THE *MESSENGER.*

IS THERE, *LUIGI?*

"MESSENGER"...?

WHO--WHO *ARE* YOU? HOW DO YOU KNOW MY *NAME...?*

I KNOW ALL *SORTS* OF THINGS. FOR EXAMPLE, I KNOW ABOUT THE *GIRLS...*

I KNOW ABOUT THE *KNIFE...*

AND I KNOW WHAT YOU'VE GOT LOCKED IN THAT *ROOM.*

"THE ONLY WAY TO GET RID OF TEMPTATION IS TO YIELD TO IT." OSCAR WILDE.

THAT'S WHAT THE ROOM'S ALL ABOUT, ENNIT?

THAT IS A *GROSS MISREPRESENTATION* OF THE HOLY SACRAMENT OF...OF *CORPOREAL CONFESSION*--

SI, DESIDERA?

UH, DUE BIRRE, UH... PER FAVORE. CHEERS, LUV.

YOU WERE SAYING, PADRE...?

IN THE ROOM, THE *TEMPTATIONS* OF THE *FLESH* ARE *DRAWN OUT* AND--AND *ACTED* UPON, THAT WE MAY COME TO *BETTER UNDERSTAND* OUR *SINFUL NATURES.*

ONLY *THEN* COMES PENANCE, AND ABSOLUTION.

OH, I KNOW ALL ABOUT THE *PENANCE,* MATE. THE FLESH IS EVIL AND MUST BE *PUNISHED.*

AND IF THE ONE DOING THE PUNISHING JUST HAPPENS TO BE SOME CATHOLIC-SCHOOL DROPOUT WITH LATEX THIGH BOOTS AND A RIDING CROP--WELL, WHERE'S THE HARM IN *THAT,* EH?

IT--IT IS NOT LIKE THAT AT ALL! THE *ROOM* WAS *SET APART* FROM THE WORLD BY *PAPAL DECREE!* WHATEVER TAKES PLACE IN THERE, IT IS *NO SIN...*

NOT IN THE *ROOM.*

"*NOTHING IS FORBIDDEN, EVERYTHING IS PERMITTED.*" SOUNDS LIKE MY KINDA PLACE...

'CEPT, D'YOU KNOW *WHICH* POPE IT WAS WHO "*SET THAT ROOM APART FROM THE WORLD,*" AS YOU PUT IT? *POPE ALEXANDER VI...*

...OTHER-WISE KNOWN AS *RODERIC LLANCOL DE BORGIA.*

21

"NO. BUT THE MOMENT I SAW HER, I...I KNEW SHE WAS NOT LIKE THE OTHERS. HER EYES, HER HAIR...

"AND WHEN SHE LOOKED AT ME, I WAS...

TEMPTED?

LOST.

"WE WENT BACK TO THE ROOM AND WE--WE *DREW OUT* MY TEMPTATION. *EXORCISED* MY *LUST.*

"THE *SECRET SACRAMENT* OF *CORPOREAL CONFESSION.*"

YOU MEAN YOU FUCKED LIKE BUNNIES.

YES.

AND THEN-- LET ME TAKE A WILD GUESS.

IT ALL WENT HORRIBLY WRONG.

...YES.

"SHE BECAME...ABUSIVE. *FERAL*. SHE *MOCKED* ME, CALLED ME A *HYPOCRITE*. THREATENED TO *EXPOSE* THE SECRET SACRAMENT!

"I TRIED TO DRAG HER *AWAY*, BUT SHE WOULDN'T LEAVE THE *ROOM*. SHE WOULDN'T STOP *SCREAMING*. AND SUDDENLY THERE WAS--

"THERE WAS A *KNIFE* AND--

"OH GOD..."

BUT SHE DIDN'T--

SHE WOULDN'T--

WHY WOULDN'T SHE *DIE*?

IS THAT ALL YOU'VE GOT, YOU LITTLE PUSSY?

STICK IT IN ME AGAIN!

24

LISTEN.

THAT ROOM IS NO LONGER OF THIS WORLD--WHICH MEANS IT'S SLIGHTLY CLOSER TO CERTAIN *OTHER* PLACES I COULD MENTION.

CLOSE ENOUGH FOR SOMETHING TO GET ITS *HOOKS* INTO THE GIRL-- AND *SUMMON ITSELF* INTO HER.

YOUR *LUST* AND *GUILT* DREW IT LIKE A *FLY* TO *SHIT.*

BUT WHAT... WHAT *IS* IT?

WHAT ELSE? A *SUCCUBUS.*

YOU'VE ONLY GONE AND LET A *SEX DEMON* LOOSE IN THE *VATICAN,* YOU *FUCKING NITWIT!*

OH, GOD! I HAVE *DAMNED* MYSELF--!

NOT *YET,* YOU HAVEN'T.

WHATEVER HAPPENS IN THAT ROOM *STAYS* IN THAT ROOM. NOTHING YOU EVER DID IN THERE CAN BE CONSIDERED A SIN IN THE EYES OF GOD--LUCKILY FOR YOU.

BUT IF THAT THING GETS *OUT*--WELL, THAT'S ANOTHER STORY.

THEN AN *EXORCISM*--

WON'T WORK--NOT BEFORE WE *DEACTIVATE* THE *WARD* ON THE ROOM. AND IN ORDER TO DO THAT, WE'LL HAVE TO *REVERSE* THE SPELL *BORGIA* USED.

FORTUNATELY, IT'S IN ONE OF THE *LOST GOSPELS.* HERE, I'LL WRITE DOWN THE TITLE SO YOU DON'T FORGET IT...

THE-- THERE IS NO SUCH BOOK!

YES THERE IS, AND YOU BLOODY WELL KNOW IT.

IT'S LOCKED UP IN THE VATICAN'S BLACK LIBRARY--AND *YOU'RE* GOING TO *BORROW* IT FOR A COUPLE OF HOURS.

I-IMPOSSIBLE!

FOR ME, MAYBE. BUT NOT FOR YOU.

I HAPPEN TO KNOW YOU'RE ONE OF THE *BLACK LIBRARIANS.* YOU'VE GOT *ACCESS.*

THIS IS *MADNESS!* I WON'T DO IT!

FINE. GO TELL YOUR *MONSIGNOR* WHAT YOU'VE DONE, AND WE'LL SEE HOW *FORGIVING* THE HOLY SEE REALLY IS.

WHAT DO YOU THINK? PREFERABLE?

NO.

THEN *STOP WHINING* AND *MAN THE FUCK UP,* YOU BLEEDIN' INGRATE!

WE'LL SWAP THE BOOK FOR A RINGER 'TIL WE'RE DONE WITH IT.

THE YELLOW PAGES...?

I'VE PUT A GLAMOUR ON IT, THEY'LL SEE EXACTLY WHAT THEY EXPECT TO SEE.

YOU DO TRUST ME, DON'T YOU?

I...I DON'T KNOW.

THEN JUST TRUST IN THE *LORD*, LUIGI.

TRUST IN THE LORD.

I--I WILL!

DAWN IS BREAKING AS FATHER GRIMALDI HURRIES THROUGH THE INMOST PASSAGES OF THE VATICAN APOSTOLIC PALACE, THE LOWER STAFF ALREADY RISING IN PREPARATION FOR THE MATINS.

HE MUST ACT SWIFTLY, BEFORE THE *THING* IN THE ROOM IS DISCOVERED.

THE APOSTOLIC LIBRARY IS WHERE THE VATICAN'S MOST FAMOUS WORKS ARE DISPLAYED TO THE WORLD--A MAGNET FOR TOURISTS AND THE FAITHFUL ALIKE.

YET DEEP IN THE HEART OF THE PALACE ITSELF IS *ANOTHER.* THE *BLACK LIBRARY* IS WHERE THE *FORBIDDEN* KNOWLEDGE IS HIDDEN.

THE GARGOYLE WATCHES HIS APPROACH WITH EYES THAT GLINT UNBLINKING IN THE GLOOM. SILVER COFFIN-COINS, TAKEN FROM THE EYELIDS OF A LONG-DEAD SEER.

HE FEELS THEM PROBING HIS SOUL AS HE APPROACHES, EXPOSING HIS INMOST SELF, LIKE THE EAGERLY QUESTING FINGERS OF A CHILD MOLESTER.

BUT FATHER GRIMALDI IS A BLACK LIBRARIAN. HE IS *PERMITTED*.

THE FAMILIAR SCENT OF LEATHER AND PARCHMENT GREETS HIM.

GUARDIAN MAGICS WHISPER IN THE GLOOM, MANY EVOKED FROM THE VERY GRIMOIRES THIS LIBRARY WAS BUILT TO CONTAIN.

UNLIKE THEIR AUTHORS, THESE BOOKS WERE NEVER BURNED.

FATHER GRIMALDI KNOWS FULL WELL WHAT HAPPENS TO THOSE WHO TRESPASS AGAINST THIS PLACE.

GIVEN A TINY GLIMPSE OF THE DAMNATION THAT AWAITS THEM, SOME ARE DRIVEN MAD WITH HORROR.

OTHERS FIND THEM-SELVES COMPELLED TO SUDDEN AND VIOLENT SUICIDE.

HE WALKS THE RAZOR'S EDGE.

ELECTRIC WITH FEAR, HE PASSES SILENTLY BETWEEN THE DUSTY SHELVES--NOT DARING TOUCH THEM, LEST SOME POTENT SPARK OF HIS INTENTION SHOULD GROUND ITSELF THROUGH THEM AND STOP HIS HEART, OR SHATTER HIM LIKE GLASS.

HE FINDS THE MASTER LIBRARIAN MONSIGNOR ROSSI'S STUDY EMPTY, AND, SENSING SOME GREATER FORCE AT WORK THAN MERE COINCIDENCE, WHISPERS A TINY PRAYER OF THANKS.

IT CANNOT BE CALLED THEFT, FOR HIS HAND IS GUIDED BY A HIGHER POWER.

THE CHURCH IS GOD'S INSTRUMENT ON THIS EARTH, AND IT MUST BE PROTECTED AT ALL COSTS--EVEN FROM ITSELF.

KNOWLEDGE IS POWER, AND THE MOST DANGEROUS BOOKS ARE CAGED LIKE JUNGLE BEASTS.

SOME ARE BOUND IN THE SKIN OF THEIR AUTHORS, FLAYED FROM THEIR LIVING FLESH BY SKILLFUL INTERROGATORS...

BUT NOT THIS BOOK. IT IS ONE OF THE LOST GOSPELS THAT FATHER GRIMALDI HAS COME FOR.

THE LAST REMAINING COPY OF A HERETICAL WORK PASSED DOWN THROUGH THE SHADOWS OF THE CENTURIES. ITS COVER BEARS NO TITLE, ITS VERY EXISTENCE DENIED.

FATHER GRIMALDI HAS HEARD WHISPERS OF THE BLASPHEMIES IT CONTAINS, ALBEIT NOTHING TO THE PURPOSE OF WHICH THE ENGLISHMAN SPOKE...

NO MATTER. HE KNOWS HE IS LOST IN MYSTERY NOW, HIS PATH ALREADY SET. PUTTING HIS TRUST IN THE LORD, HE SLIPS THE HIDDEN CARGO FROM HIS CASSOCK.

THE STARK YELLOW COVER OF THE TELEPHONE DIRECTORY LOOKS CRASS AND GARISH IN THIS RAREFIED PLACE.

PAGINE GIALLE

THE ENGLISHMAN SAID HE HAD PUT A SPELL UPON IT.

A FEW DAYS AGO, FATHER GRIMALDI WOULD HAVE SCOFFED AT THE MERE SUGGESTION. BUT NOW HE HAS WITNESSED MIRACLES, AND HORRORS, BEYOND HIS OWN IMAGINING, AND HE *BELIEVES.*

YET HOW, HE WONDERS, COULD SOMETHING SO VULGAR EVER BE MISTAKEN FOR--

FATHER GRIMALDI.

MONSIGNOR ROSSI! YOU--YOU *STARTLED* ME.

THE *HIDDEN* ROOM, OF COURSE. I UNDERSTAND YOU HAVE TAKEN IT UPON YOURSELF TO UNDERTAKE CERTAIN *RENOVATIONS.*

OH! YES! THE RENOVATIONS ARE PROGRESSING WELL. YOU REALLY, *UH...*

YOU WOULDN'T RECOGNIZE IT.

SHOW ME.

...WHAT?

YOU HAVE BEEN *MOST* ATTENTIVE, LUIGI, TAKING IT UPON YOURSELF TO CARE FOR OUR MOST GUARDED SECRETS. I SEE I WAS RIGHT TO BRING YOU INTO MY TRUST.

NOW LET'S GO AND SEE THESE RENOVATIONS. I'M SURE YOU'LL BE WORTHY OF SOME *REWARD.*

IT...IT'S NOT QUITE FINISHED YET.

COME NOW, LUIGI... NO NEED FOR MODESTY.

ALL THE WAY THROUGH THE PALACE, FATHER GRIMALDI'S MIND RACES IN SEARCH OF AN EXCUSE TO KEEP THE MASTER LIBRARIAN FROM THE ROOM.

BUT HIS MIND IS BLANK, HIS FACULTIES BEREFT. A RABBIT IN THE HEAD-LIGHTS, POWERLESS IN THE FACE OF THE INEVITABLE.

THE ENGLISHMAN, HE TELLS HIMSELF. THE ENGLISHMAN WILL THINK OF SOMETHING.

BUT AS THEY APPROACH THE ROOM, FATHER GRIMALDI CLUTCHES THE STOLEN BOOK TIGHTER BENEATH HIS CASSOCK AS HE REALIZES THE ENGLISHMAN HAS *GONE.*

HE IS ALONE, WITH NO MORE GUILE LEFT IN HIM--ONLY *DESPERATION.*

WHAT IS THIS...?

DON'T.

...I BEG YOUR PARDON?

MONSIGNORE, FORGIVE ME, BUT--

DON'T... DON'T OPEN THE DOOR.

WHAT DO YOU SAY, LOVERBOY-- READY TO GO AGAIN?

IT'S NOT OVER, LITTLE PRIEST!

YOUR GOD WILL NOT FORGIVE YOU FOR WHAT YOU HAVE DONE! HE WILL NEVER FORGIVE YOU--!

MY GOD *IS* FORGIVENESS.

AMEN.

EXORCISO TE, IMMUNDISSIME SPIRITUS, OMNIS INCURSIO ADVERSARII, OMNE PHANTASMA, OMNIS LEGIO, IN NOMINE DOMINI NOSTRI JESU CHRISTI ERADICARE, ET EFFUGARE AB HOC PLASMATE DEI!

AND WITH THAT, THE ENGLISHMAN IS GONE--AS IF HE HAD NEVER BEEN THERE.

FATHER GRIMALDI KNOWS HE HAS ONLY TO RETURN THE LOST GOSPEL TO THE BLACK LIBRARY, AND HIS ORDEAL IS OVER.

PAGINE GIALLE

PAGINE GIALLE

PAGINE GIALLE

PAGINE GIALLE

OH, SHIT!

"WE MEET AGAIN, MY OLD ADVERSARY!"

FUCK'S SAKE, ELLIE, WHERE'D YOU GET THAT LINE FROM? I COULD BARELY KEEP A STRAIGHT FACE!

LOOK WHO'S TALKING, YOU OLD HAM.

I MEAN, "DO YOUR WORST, HELL SPAWN"? REALLY?

YEAH, WELL, IT'S THE VATICAN, ENNIT? THEY DON'T REALLY DO SUBTLE.

DID THE TRICK, THOUGH, DIDN'T IT?

THEY LEAD *THEMSELVES* ASTRAY. THAT'S WHY THEY BOUGHT INTO BORGIA'S COCK AND BULL STORY IN THE FIRST PLACE, ISN'T IT?

THEY *LOVE* TO THINK THERE'S A PLACE WHERE GOD CAN'T STAND IN *JUDGMENT* OF THEM. AS IF HE'S EVEN PAYING *ATTENTION.*

THEY DAMN *THEMSELVES.*

YEAH.

I THINK WE ALL DO, LUV.

POOR LITTLE JOHN.

BLOODY HELL, ELLIE! WHAT WAS THAT IN AID OF...?

SUCCUBUS 101.

ALWAYS LEAVE 'EM WANTING MORE.

SO THERE WAS THIS BLOKE, RIGHT?

AGIOS NIKOLAUS HIS NAME WAS, BORN IN A.D. 270 IN PATARA, LYCIA. THAT'S PART OF TURKEY TODAY, BUT BACK THEN IT WAS A GREEK-SPEAKING PROVINCE OF THE ROMAN EMPIRE.

BY THAT POINT, WORSHIP OF THE OLD ROMAN GODS HAD GRADUALLY WANED IN FAVOR OF SOL INVICTUS, THE "UNCONQUERED SUN," BORN WITH A HALO OF LIGHT ON DECEMBER 25TH.

THE STORY OF JESUS WAS ALREADY SPREADING AROUND THE MEDITERRANEAN LIKE A DOSE OF THE CLAP, AND THE ROMAN EMPEROR CONSTANTINE DIDN'T NEED A WEATHER-VANE TO SEE WHICH WAY THE WIND BLOWS.

SO HE DECREED THAT CHRISTIANITY BECOME THE OFFICIAL STATE RELIGION OF THE ROMAN EMPIRE, CANNILY COMBINING THE EXISTING--ALBEIT CONTRADICTORY--ACCOUNTS OF THE LIFE OF JESUS WITH THE MYTHOLOGY OF SOL INVICTUS...

...JUST TO SWEETEN THE PILL FOR THE PROLES, YOU UNDERSTAND.

IF THAT DATE SOUNDS SUSPICIOUSLY FAMILIAR, BEAR WITH ME. IT GETS BETTER.

NOW THIS *AGIOS NIKOLAUS*--THE TURKISH BLOKE, YEAH? PAY ATTENTION--

--HE WAS SUBSEQUENTLY APPOINTED *BISHOP OF MYRA*, WHERE HE EARNED A GLOWING REPUTATION FOR *CHARITY, BENEVOLENCE* AND *ANONYMOUS GIFT-GIVING*...

...NOT TO MENTION THE ODD *MIRACLE* HERE AND THERE. RESURRECTING MURDERED KIDS WHO'D BEEN TURNED INTO MINCE PIES, THAT SORT OF THING.

QUITE THE PARTY PIECE, IT MUST HAVE BEEN.

REVERED AS A *SAINT* AFTER HIS DEATH IN A.D. 343, HIS REMAINS WERE ENTOMBED IN MYRA--UNTIL THE SARACENS INVADED IN THE 11TH CENTURY...

...WHEREUPON THE FAITHFUL SHIPPED HIS BONES OVER TO THE *BASILICA DI SAN NICOLA* IN BARI, ITALY...

...WHERE THEY REMAIN TO THIS DAY.

AS I LIVE AND BREATHE. CLARICE SACKVILLE, RUNNING TOWARDS THE SOUND OF GUNFIRE.

YOU HEARD THE CALL THEN?

EVERY SENSITIVE IN *LONDON* MUST HAVE HEARD IT. A CRY FOR HELP FROM THE HEART OF A DYING MAGE.

I SAW IT IN *DREAM* IMAGERY. A *SHARK*, DEVOURING ALL IN ITS PATH.

I DON'T KNOW WHY I CAME. I SHOULD RETURN TO MY ORDER AND LOCK THE GATES.

NO, BROTHER CHALICE. I'D SAY YOUR INSTINCTS ARE SOUND...

HEH. THAT GOES AGAINST THE GRAIN.

DO YOU KNOW WHAT IT IS?

NO. IT IS CONCEALING ITSELF.

ALL I KNOW IS THAT IF WE *RUN*...

WHATEVER THIS THING IS THAT'S BEEN SLAUGHTERING ITS WAY THROUGH THE MAGICKAL UNDERWORLD, IT'S CLEARLY TAPPED INTO A SOURCE OF *TERRIFYING* POWER.

NONE OF US ARE STRONG ENOUGH TO DEFEAT IT ALONE.

WE MUST STAND *UNITED.*

FOR GOD'S SAKE, MAKO! YOU'VE GOT *BLOOD* ON YOU...

YOU SHOULD SEE THE INSIDE OF YOUR *CAR*. I BROUGHT A LITTLE SOMETHING WITH ME FOR THE *ROAD*, EH?

I THOUGHT WE AGREED TO KEEP THINGS *LOW KEY*. THIS IS *ENGLAND*. YOU CAN'T JUST GO AROUND *CANNIBALIZING V.I.P.'S* AND NOT EXPECT THE *AUTHORITIES* TO NOTICE--

FUCK THEM. YOU *ARE* THE AUTHORITIES. YOU ARE A *LORD*, YOU MAKE THE LAW, *EH*?

NEVERTHELESS, THERE ARE CERTAIN... *APPEARANCES* TO BE KEPT UP. *PRETENCES* TO BE MAINTAINED.

BESIDES, YOUR POWERS HAVE MULTIPLIED A *THOUSANDFOLD*. THERE'S SIMPLY NO *NEED* FOR YOU TO CONTINUE THIS MINDLESS SLAUGHTER OF MAGES.

YOU HAVE *ENOUGH* POWER.

THERE IS NO SUCH THING.

HEH. WE ARE NOT SO UNALIKE AFTER ALL, ARE WE, YOU AND I?

I MYSELF HAVE DEDICATED MY LIFE TO THE ACQUISITION OF POWER IN ALL ITS FORMS--AND HERE, AT THE END, I HAVE COME UP HARD AGAINST THE *LIMITS* OF THAT POWER.

NUCLEAR POWER? YOU TRYING TO SAVE THE PLANET, *EH?*

YOU CAN'T IMAGINE THE TIME AND RESOURCES I'VE POURED INTO THE SEARCH FOR *IMMORTALITY.* BUT ALL IN VAIN.

OH, FUCK THE PLANET. THE PLANET IS *DOOMED.* THEY'LL BE EATING EACH OTHER IN THE STREETS WITHIN A GENERATION, YOU MARK MY WORDS.

NO, THIS IS ALL JUST... A MEANS TO AN END.

MY END, SPECIFICALLY.

MY TIME LEFT ON THIS MORTAL COIL GROWS SHORT...

...AND I KNOW *EXACTLY* WHAT AWAITS ME ON THE *OTHER* SIDE...

DANGER
Radiation

184

...THANKS TO *THIS.*

AND WHY SUFFER THE TORMENTS OF *HELL* WHEN YOU CAN CREATE YOUR *OWN PRIVATE HEAVEN*, EH?

EXACTLY SO. WHICH IS WHERE *YOU* COME IN, MY FRIEND.

I UPHELD MY SIDE OF THE BARGAIN. I GAVE YOU ACCESS TO THE HELL MIRROR, AND YOU HAVE FUELED YOUR *MUTI* MAGIC WITH THE AGONIES OF THE DAMNED.

NOW IT'S TIME, AS THE SAYING GOES, TO PAY THE PIPER.

OPEN IT.

THIS FACILITY WILL KEEP THE *SOUL CAGE* SAFE AND SECURE AS IT HOUSES MY IMMORTAL SOUL, THUS NEATLY BYPASSING ANY...*INFERNAL UNPLEASANTRIES.*

...AND THEN... I SHALL KILL MYSELF.

AFTER TRANSFERRING THE MIRROR TO YOURSELF, OF COURSE.

BUT NEEDLESS TO SAY, I HAVE NO INTENTION OF SPENDING ETERNITY IN AN *EMPTY VOID*.

YOU WILL *FURNISH* THE VOID WITH A *PALACE* OF SUCH *OPULENCE* AS TO RIVAL THE FABLED PLEASURE DOME OF *KUBLA KHAN* HIMSELF, POPULATED WITH *HOURIS* TO SATISFY EVERY PROCLIVITY AND PERVERSION...

HMM.

BE SURE THAT YOU DO, OLD MAN...

...OR YOUR SOUL WILL NEVER SEE THE PALACE.

I'D STOLEN THE GOSPEL OF CONSTANTINE LOOKING FOR AN ANGLE ON THAT WHOLE LAUGHING MAGICIAN DEBACLE...

...BUT WHEN IT POINTED ME TO THE *GRAVE* OF *OLD SAINT NICK* HIMSELF--WELL, A CRAZY LITTLE IDEA SNUCK INTO MY HEAD AND RESOLUTELY REFUSED TO SNEAK OUT AGAIN.

PLENTY OF MAGICIANS USE SOME KIND OF GIMMICK TO CHANNEL POWER, OR FOCUS THEIR OWN.

BLOOD, BONES, TAROT, CRYSTALS. YOU NAME IT.

SO IT WOULD SEEM. YOU WALK THE *SYNCHRONICITY HIGHWAY,* DANCING BETWEEN THE RAINDROPS-- APPEARING WHERE YOU ARE NEEDED, ALWAYS IN THE RIGHT PLACE AT THE RIGHT TIME...

BUT HAS IT NEVER OCCURRED TO YOU TO QUESTION *WHY?*

NEVER BEEN ONE TO LOOK A GIFT HORSE IN THE MOUTH, ME.

BUT STILL. JUST LATELY...I DUNNO. EVER SINCE I'VE TRIED TO GET MY *SHIT* BACK TOGETHER, IT FEELS LIKE SOMEONE'S TRYING TO STEER ME BACK INTO THE *FOG.*

DON'T SUPPOSE *YOU'D* KNOW ANYTHING ABOUT THAT, WOULD YOU...?

I CANNOT SEE. THERE IS A SHADOW ABOUT YOU.

YEAH, I KNOW-- AND THAT'S SOMETHING *ELSE* THAT BOTHERS ME.

BUT I'M ABOUT TO TAP INTO A POWER SOURCE OF ME *OWN*--AND *THEN* I'LL BE ABLE TO SEE HOW I *REALLY* FIT INTO THE GRAND SCHEME OF THINGS.

YOU ARE PLAYING WITH *FIRE,* CONSTANTINE.

YEAH, WELL.

I NEEDED A *LIGHT.*

EVEN THE *ATHEISTS* KNOW, DEEP DOWN INSIDE THEMSELVES IN A PLACE THEY'D NEVER ADMIT TO, THERE'S SOMETHING *MAGIC* ABOUT THIS TIME OF YEAR...

...BELIEVING IT MAKES IT TRUE.

BUT CHRISTMAS ISN'T ABOUT CHRIST IN THIS DAY AND AGE.

IF THERE'S ONE FIGURE THAT DOMINATES THE POPULAR PERCEPTION OF CHRISTMAS MAGIC, IT'S JOLLY OLD *SANTA.*

THANKS TO THE JOYS OF *MASS CONSUMERISM,* SANTA'S BECOME A *FOLK ICON* OF LITERALLY *MYTHIC* PROPORTIONS.

THAT'S A LOT OF *BELIEF.*

A LOT OF *POWER*...

AND JUST LIKE THAT, I'M PLUGGED INTO THE MAIN SOURCE.

ELECTRIC WITH ENERGY. LIT UP LIKE BLOODY *OXFORD STREET* ON *CHRISTMAS EVE*...

IT'S ALMOST TOO MUCH. OVERWHELMING, A TIDAL WAVE OF *RAW POWER* THREATENING TO *ENGULF* ME...

BUT IT'S NOT MY FIRST WHITE-KNUCKLE HEAD TRIP. I CAN RIDE IT OUT. HANG ON TIGHT AND GO WITH THE FLOW.

AND EVENTUALLY THE TIDAL WAVE SETTLES AND I'M *FLOATING* FACE-UP IN A SEA OF ENERGY. PURE, UNREFINED *BELIEF*.

IT'S *INTOXICATING.* I COULD GET *USED* TO THIS...

NO. *FOCUS,* JOHN...

YOU CAN'T *SEE* ME, CAN YOU, MAKO...?

BUT I CAN SEE *YOU*.

EVERYTHING'S BEEN PREPARED ACCORDING TO YOUR INSTRUCTIONS, LORD BURNHAM.

JUST THESE LAST FEW SIGNATURES, AND THE TRUST WILL BE EMPOWERED TO OVERSEE YOUR, UH...

NO ENTRY
AUTHORISED PERSONNEL ONLY

Brinkley Point
NUCLEAR WASTE STORAGE FACILITY
AUTHORISED PERSONNEL ONLY

MY LITTLE *NEST EGG.* VERY GOOD, WARDLOW.

YOU'VE DONE WELL, AND YOUR REWARD IS WAITING IN YOUR SWISS ACCOUNT AS AGREED.

SO, IS MAKO... *INSIDE?*

I ASKED HIM TO MAKE SOME FINAL MODIFICATIONS TO THE *HAREM.* IF I'M TO SPEND ETERNITY *ABUSING* THEM, I WANT TO MAKE SURE THEY'LL MAINTAIN MY INTEREST.

AS SOON AS HE EMERGES, I'LL TURN THIS TAP AND, WELL...

...PASS ACROSS.

WILL IT...

WILL IT *HURT?*

OH, QUITE THE OPPOSITE. THIS IS DIAMORPHINE. PHARMACEUTICAL HEROIN.

IT'S QUITE EASY TO GET HOLD OF IN POSITIVELY *INDUSTRIAL* QUANTITIES, SO LONG AS ONE KNOWS A CONSULTANT CARDIAC SURGEON WITH THE RIGHT... *PREDILECTIONS.*

DIAMORPHINE

I SHALL *OVERDOSE MASSIVELY* AND BE SWEPT OUT OF THIS LIFE ON A WAVE OF *BLISS...*

AND THE *SOUL CAGE* WILL CATCH ME AND COSSET ME INTO AN ETERNITY OF *EARTHLY DELIGHTS.*

I'LL BE BACK TO SEAL THE CONTAINER ONCE YOU'VE--ONCE IT'S *DONE.*

WHAT ABOUT MAKO...?

NOT MY PROBLEM ANYMORE, DEAR BOY.

JUST WATCH YOUR BACK.

YOUR LORDSHIP.

IT HAS BEEN AN HONOR TO SERVE.

IS IT DONE, MAKO? HAVE THE FINAL PREPARATIONS BEEN MADE?

...READY WHEN YOU ARE.

THEN IT'S TIME.

AAAAAHHH...

THE *SYRINGE!* NEED... ADRENALINE--

P-PLEASE...

YOU WERE IN MAKO'S *MIND.* I CAN SEE IT *ALL* NOW. ALL THE *ANGLES...*

ALL THE *LITTLE PEOPLE* YOU'VE FUCKED OVER--ALL THE *INNOCENT LIVES* YOU'VE DESTROYED-- IN YOUR SCRAMBLE FOR MONEY AND POWER AND NASTY KICKS WITHOUT CONSEQUENCES.

WELL *I'M* THE FUCKING CONSEQUENCES, SUNSHINE.

AND I'M THINKING *MAKO* WON'T BE TOO CHUFFED THAT YOU GOT HIM TRAPPED IN THAT *SOUL CAGE* FOR THE REST OF ETERNITY.

YOUR PRIVATE HEAVEN JUST TURNED INTO A PRIVATE *HELL,* MATE-- AND *MAKO'S* THE *DEVIL.*

GIVE HIM MY BEST WHEN YOU GET THERE, WON'T YOU?

A-ANYTHING... I'LL GIVE YOU ANYTHING...

I CAN MAKE YOU RICH...

YOU MADE YOUR OWN BED, BURNHAM.

FUCKIN' *LIE* IN IT.

YOU GOT OFF EASY.

WARNING
NO ADMITTANCE

LORD CALVIN BURNHAM WILL SHORTLY BE STEPPING DOWN FROM PUBLIC LIFE.

CHARITY IS ITS OWN REWARD, AND HE PREFERS TO CONTINUE SERVING THE PUBLIC TRUST BEYOND THE ATTENDANT MEDIA SPOTLIGHT THAT COMES WITH PUBLIC OFFICE.

LORD BURNHAM IS DOING, UH--

WHAT HE'S DOING IS LYING *DEAD* BACK THERE WITH A *NEEDLE* STUCK IN HIS ARM.

RICH MAN'S SMACK.

WHAT?! YOU CAN'T--

YOU PEOPLE ARE SUPPOSED TO BE *JOURNALISTS*.

STOP FILMING! TURN THOSE CAMERAS OFF--!

SECURITY! SECURITY--!

UH, THAT IS, DON'T LISTEN TO THIS MAN--

TIME WAS, THE PRESS WOULD ACTUALLY *INVESTIGATE* THE NEWS INSTEAD OF JUST RECYCLING PRESS RELEASES FROM CORPORATE MOUTHPIECES LIKE *THIS* LITTLE TOSSER.

WELL, *I'VE* GOT A FUCKING STORY FOR YOU...

BURNHAM WAS UP TO HIS FLAKY, LIVER-SPOTTED SCALP IN NASTY SHIT, AND *MAKO*--THAT IS, I WAS HIS *MUSCLE*.

LOOK AT THE CHAN CHU RESTAURANT MASSACRE. HUNGER HILL. ERIC GREGGS. LYCHGATE.

THE STORY'S THERE. BUT YOU'LL HAVE TO *DIG* FOR IT. *LITERALLY*.

93

"BRING IT TO LIGHT, MAKE IT RIGHT"? WHAT WAS THAT, A FUCKING *CHANT*?

I SOUNDED LIKE SOME SANDAL-WEARING TREE-HUGGER ON SPEAKER'S CORNER.

SO IS THAT IT? I SHOULD BE SATISFIED, BUT...THERE'S NO SENSE OF VICTORY. NOT EVEN CLOSURE.

SOMEHOW IT ALL FEELS HOLLOW. EMPTY.

SOMETHING'S MISSING. THE PIECE OF THE JIGSAW THAT MAKES IT ALL MAKE SENSE.

IT'S ALL COME TOGETHER A BIT TOO CLEAN FOR MY LIKING. THE WARNING FROM AFRICA. THE GOSPEL OF CONSTANTINE. THE POWER OF SAINT NICK...

ALL RIGHT, SO COINCIDENCE, SYNCHRONICITY, WHATEVER YOU WANNA CALL IT--IT'S ALWAYS LINED UP FOR ME AND I'VE NEVER REALLY *QUESTIONED* IT...

...UNTIL NOW.

FUCK IT.

FUCK SYNCHRONICITY.

FUCK COINCIDENCE.

TAXI!

I'M ME OWN MAN, AND I GO ME OWN WAY. NOBODY'S PULLING *MY* STRINGS--

BLOODY 'ELL-- JOHN!

AND THERE'S ME THINKIN' YOU'D BIN *AVOIDIN'* ME LATELY.

...CHAS?

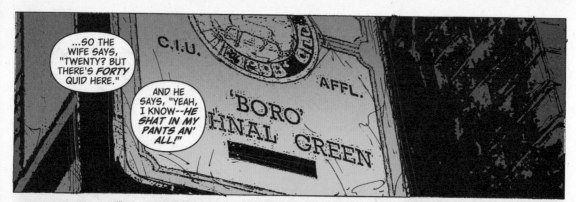

...SO THE WIFE SAYS, "TWENTY? BUT THERE'S *FORTY* QUID HERE."

AND HE SAYS, "YEAH, I KNOW--*HE SHAT IN MY PANTS AN' ALL!*"

AHH HA HA HA HA HA HA HAAAHHH HAH HA

AAH, JESUS, I NEEDED THAT. BEEN A WHILE SINCE I HAD A GOOD LAUGH, ENNIT?

YEAH, WELL, WHOSE FAULT'S THAT? YOU BEEN A STRANGER EVER SINCE WE GOT BACK FROM THAT BOLLOCKS UP IN SCOTLAND.

OI! FUCK'S SAKE, JOHN! I'M STILL PAYING FOR THIS MOTOR--!

LET IT GO, CHAS, I'M NOT IN THE MOOD. JUST GIMME A WIDE BERTH 'TIL I'VE GOT THIS SORTED, YEAH?

I'M DRIVING THE *WRONG WAY* UP THE *SYNCHRONICITY* HIGHWAY...

AND *SOMEONE'S* TRYING TO MAKE *DAMN SURE* I DON'T MAKE IT TO THE OTHER END.

AAAH!

THE BACKLASH KNOCKED ME FLAT ON MY ARSE, WHICH SHOULD HAVE BEEN A DEAD GIVEAWAY.

BUT WHATEVER IT WAS THE SPELL BROUGHT TO LIGHT...

...IT CAME OUT OF ME.

OI! WHO'S THERE...?

I ONLY CAUGHT A GLIMPSE OF IT, SCURRYING FOR THE COVER OF DARKNESS LIKE A COCKROACH...

BUT IT LOOKED LIKE A MAN.

NOT A LITTLE GIRL WITH HER ARM TORN OFF.

NOT A SHAPELESS INSANITY-THING.

A MAN.

AND IN THAT BRIEF MOMENT THE FIGURE STOOD REVEALED, MAKO CAUGHT A *GLIMPSE* OF IT FROM HALF A WORLD AWAY.

I SAW A CAGE OF MIRRORS. A RAVEN AND A SCAR.

AND THEN I SAW *HIM.* JUST FOR A MOMENT. BUT HIS FACE WAS HIDDEN FROM ME, A FLEEING SHADOW...

AND THEN HE WAS GONE.

HE FOLLOWED IT TO ENGLAND, THINKING IT WAS *ME.*

BUT IT HAD *HIDDEN* AGAIN. THROWN A *CLOAKING SPELL* AROUND ITSELF--AND *ME* WITH IT.

I CANNOT SEE. THERE IS A SHADOW ABOUT YOU.

BECAUSE ALL THIS TIME, IT'S BEEN HIDING IN THE *ONE PLACE* I'D NEVER THINK TO LOOK...

...*INSIDE ME.*

ALL RIGHT, YOU SLIPPERY LITTLE BUGGER.

ENOUGH OF THIS *SNEAKING AROUND* SHIT.

THE UNIVERSE PULLS THE RUG OUT FROM UNDER ME AND SUDDENLY I'M KNEELING IN *DAMP GRASS.*

IT'S THE *SMELL* THAT HITS ME FIRST. SEAWEED AND HEATHER AND SHEEP SHIT. THE SMELL OF THE *COUNTRY.*

THEN THE SOUNDS. THE ROAR OF THE SEA. THE LONELY CRIES OF GULLS.

AND EVEN BEFORE I OPEN MY EYES, I *KNOW* WHERE I AM.

RAVENSCAR.

IT ALWAYS COMES BACK TO RAVENSCAR, DUNNIT?

THE WALLS ALWAYS *WERE* THIN HERE.

THE WALLS BETWEEN *WORLDS.*

HELLO, JOHN.

YEAH? SO IF *YOU'RE* THE *LAUGHING MAGICIAN,* WHAT DOES THAT MAKE *ME...?*

SLOPPY SECONDS?

PUT ASIDE YOUR JEALOUSY AND RESENTMENT, JOHN. YOU AND I *RECONCILED* LONG AGO.

DO YOU *REMEMBER...?*

VAGUELY. BUT IT WAS BLOODY *YEARS* AGO...

I WAS OFF MY *TITS* ON *MAGIC MUSHROOMS* AT THE TIME, AND NOTHING SEEMED TO HAVE CHANGED AFTERWARDS. I FIGURED IT WAS JUST A *BAD TRIP.*

THAT WAS *REAL?*

AS REAL AS ANY OF THIS. WE *MERGED OUR SOULS,* YOU AND I. BECAME *AS ONE...*

...EXCEPT, OF COURSE, THAT WE *DIDN'T...*

"...YOUR *EGO* WAS TOO *STRONG,* YOU SEE. YOUR SOUL RESISTED, UNWILLING TO SACRIFICE ITSELF FOR THE GREATER GOOD.

"AND SO OUR SOULS *SEPARATED* AGAIN, LIKE OIL AND WATER.

"AND I REMAINED, A VESTIGIAL TWIN, FORGOTTEN AND IGNORED, ENTOMBED WITHIN ITS OWN BUBBLE REALITY HIDDEN DEEP WITHIN YOUR SOUL."

AND YOU'VE BEEN HERE EVER SINCE, HAVEN'T YOU?

THAT NAGGING LITTLE FEELING AT THE BACK OF MY MIND. THE *ITCH* I COULD NEVER *SCRATCH.*

I HAVE BEEN WATCHING OVER YOU. WATCHING, AND WAITING, UNTIL YOU HAD GROWN WISE ENOUGH, *SELFLESS* ENOUGH, THAT YOUR SOUL MIGHT NO LONGER *REJECT* ME. THAT WE MIGHT TRULY *MERGE*...

AND I COULD FINALLY BE BORN INTO *YOUR* WORLD. IN *YOU.*

NOW IS THE TIME. YOU ARE *READY.*

JOIN WITH ME, JOHN, AND LET US FULLFIL OUR BIRTHRIGHT.

THE SECRETS OF THE UNIVERSE WILL BE OURS TO SHARE.

THE POWER OF THE *LAUGHING MAGICIAN* WILL BE OURS TO SHARE.

YOU NEED ONLY... *LET GO.*

LET GO...?

OF YOUR *EGO.* YOUR OVERRIDING SENSE OF *SELF.*

STEP OFF. LET YOUR OLD SELF *FALL AWAY.*

YOU WILL BE *REBORN* IN ME, OUR SOULS COMBINED, OUR EYES OPEN TO INFINITIES AS YET UNIMAGINED.

FUCK IT.

I GO ME OWN WAY.

ALWAYS HAVE.

THE END